Too Cool

Skateboard Standout

Phil Kettle
illustrated by Craig Smith

Black Hills

Black Hills Publishing Pty Ltd
433 Wellington Street
Clifton Hill
Melbourne AUSTRALIA 3068

www.kidzbookhub.com.au
office@kidzbookhub.com.au

All rights reserved. No part of this publication may be reproduced or transmitted in any form or by any means, electronic or mechanical, including photocopying, recording, storage in an information retrieval system, or otherwise, without the written permission of the publisher, unless specifically permitted under the Australian Copyright Act 1968 as amended.

ISBN: 9781920924058

 A catalogue record for this book is available from the National Library of Australia

Contents

Chapter 1
The Design — 1

Chapter 2
The Gear — 5

Chapter 3
A Long Way Down — 13

Chapter 4
The TC Twist — 18

Chapter 5
Down It Comes — 24

Toocool's Skateboard Glossary — 29
Toocool's Backyard Ramp — 30
Toocool's Quick Summary — 32
The Skateboard — 34
Q & A with Toocool — 36
Skateboard Quiz — 40

Toocool

Mr. Lopez

Scott

Dog

Chapter 1
The Design

Scott and I took our sketches out to the garage. We were going to build the coolest skateboard ramp ever.

Mom thought it was a great idea.

"Boys, I think that is a great idea. Stay outside as long as you want."

Scott and I had skated all the paths around TC Park.

We had even tied Dog to our skateboards. He towed us around. It was awesome. Unfortunately, we were still not going fast enough to do tricks.

Then we thought of the backyard. It was a good place for a skateboarding ramp.

The ramp would go from the top of the picnic table, down to the ground, then up to the top of the doghouse.

There was plenty of wood and metal in the toolshed—everything we needed.

Scott drew the design.
I had read all the top skateboarding magazines.
I gave advice.

Scott said the ramp should be named after him. He said the person who designs it, names it. Give me a break! Whoever heard of a Scott Ramp?

We got busy building.

Chapter 2
The Gear

Mr. Lopez stepped through the gap in the fence.

"Toocool, that skateboard of yours is a ticket to the hospital."

That was a strange thing to say. I think he just wanted to ride on my skateboard.

I told him about my plans to be the best extreme-action skateboarding star the world has ever seen.

Mr. Lopez scratched his chin.

He said we'd better get some safety gear.

I wrote *Skateboard Standout* on my bike helmet.

I used the cushions from the living room couch for kneepads. Dad's gardening gloves looked totally professional.

Scott put on his safety gear. He looked like a man from outer space.

We got our skateboards out and oiled the trucks.

Scott had mud all over his deck. I told him that dirt slows you down.

He just ignored me.

Bert the Rooster was on top of the garage. He wanted a bird's eye view of the action.

I could not see Dog anywhere. He was not in his house. He was not under the porch.

Dog loved to watch this kind of action, but he was going to miss out this time. I had no time to look for him.

It was time to test our need for speed. It was time to test our skills. It was time to test the Scott Ramp.

Mr. Lopez was still watching.

"Shall I call the ambulance now?" he said.

Scott asked him if he would judge the contest. He said he would.

I asked him if he would call the skateboarding magazines.

He said, "Next time."

We were going to take three turns each. Mr. Lopez would give us points out of ten for each of our turns.

I made the announcement.

"Welcome to the U.S. Skateboarding Championships. You are about to see some serious boarding. Please do not try this at home!"

The stage was set for an awesome contest.

Chapter 3
A Long Way Down

We climbed to the top of the picnic table. We went to the lip of the ramp. We looked down. The bowl was steeper than we'd planned.

We looked at each other. We both said, "You go first."

"It's called the Scott Ramp," I said to Scott, "so you go first."

"It's your backyard," he responded. "You go first."

"Okay," I said. "Watch and learn."

I adjusted my gear.
My helmet needed tightening.
My kneepads were slipping.
My gloves were a little big.

"Hurry up, Toocool!" shouted Mr. Lopez. "We haven't got all day."

I took a deep breath and pushed off—down the bowl and up the other side.

My speed was building. I was sure there was smoke coming from the trucks.

I shot up the other side and did a great ollie, then up to the lip for a nose grind.

What a ride!

"Time," yelled Mr. Lopez.

"How many points?" I asked.

"Six out of ten," Mr. Lopez said. I thought I should have gotten at least nine.

Chapter 4
The TC Twist

Scott took his turn. He did two ollies, but his nose grind wasn't very good.

Mr. Lopez gave him eight points. I could not believe it!

I did not say a thing.

Now I was even more determined to win.

I focused on what I had to do. This was going to be the greatest ride ever.

Where were the cameras when you needed them?

I pushed off, using all my strength. I picked up speed in an instant.

I had never gone faster.

I went down the bowl and up the other side. I got set to do my new trick.

Every skater wants to invent a new trick. My trick would push skateboarding into the future. It would be famous. It would be called the TC Twist.

I flew up the side of the bowl and launched myself into the air.

I must have been going too fast. I left the rim of the bowl and kept going.

I was headed straight for the gap in the fence.

Mr. Lopez's eyes bugged out! He leaped out of the way. I shot past him.

I came back down to Earth on an angle. I must have slid at least ten yards.

I took out a whole row of Mr. Lopez's tomato plants.

Chapter 5
Down It Comes

Mr. Lopez stood there with his mouth open. Scott could not stop laughing.

The chickens went wild. Bert the Rooster came down from the roof. He would not stop squawking.

Dog appeared from nowhere and started licking my face.

At last Mr. Lopez spoke.

"Toocool, are you all right? Can you move?"

I scraped squashed tomato off my face.

"Yes, sir," I mumbled. "I can move."

"Well, Toocool," he said, "I suggest that you and your skateboard and your dog *move* off my tomatoes!"

We had to pull down the Scott Ramp after that.

Mom said it took up too much space in the backyard.

Mr. Lopez said it gave him nightmares.

Dad said he needed the materials to fix the gap in the fence.

Scott and I went back to skating in TC Park. It really wasn't so bad.

When I called the skateboarding magazines, they said the world was not ready for the TC Twist.

They suggested I try a calmer sport. How about golf?

The End!

Toocool's Skateboard Glossary

Deck—The top surface of a skateboard.

Nose grind—When you grind on the front truck of the skateboard.

Ollie—This is the trick that most skateboarders should learn first. It forms the basis for other tricks. It's an easy jump trick.

Standout—Someone who does something better than anyone else.

Trucks—The trucks are attached to the skateboard and the wheels are attached to the trucks.

Toocool's Backyard Ramp

tt Ramp

Skatepark

angout

The Bert Rooster Memorial Grandstand

The Mean Streets

Toocool's Quick Summary
Skateboarding

Surfers were the first people to make skateboarding popular. When there were no waves, the surfers were looking for something to do. They decided skateboarding was the answer.

Surfing and skateboarding are alike in many ways, and skateboarders copied many of the moves that surfers used.

Skateboarders were sometimes called sidewalk surfers because skating was like surfing on the sidewalk.

Skateboarders were always looking for good places to skate. They skated around the curves of empty swimming pools, in sewer pipes, and up and down street gutters.

When skateboard parks were built, skateboarders had a great place to skate. These parks have specially designed ramps, pipes, and obstacle courses.

I don't think any of the skateboard parks have a Scott Ramp. Maybe we should send them the design!

The **Skateboard**

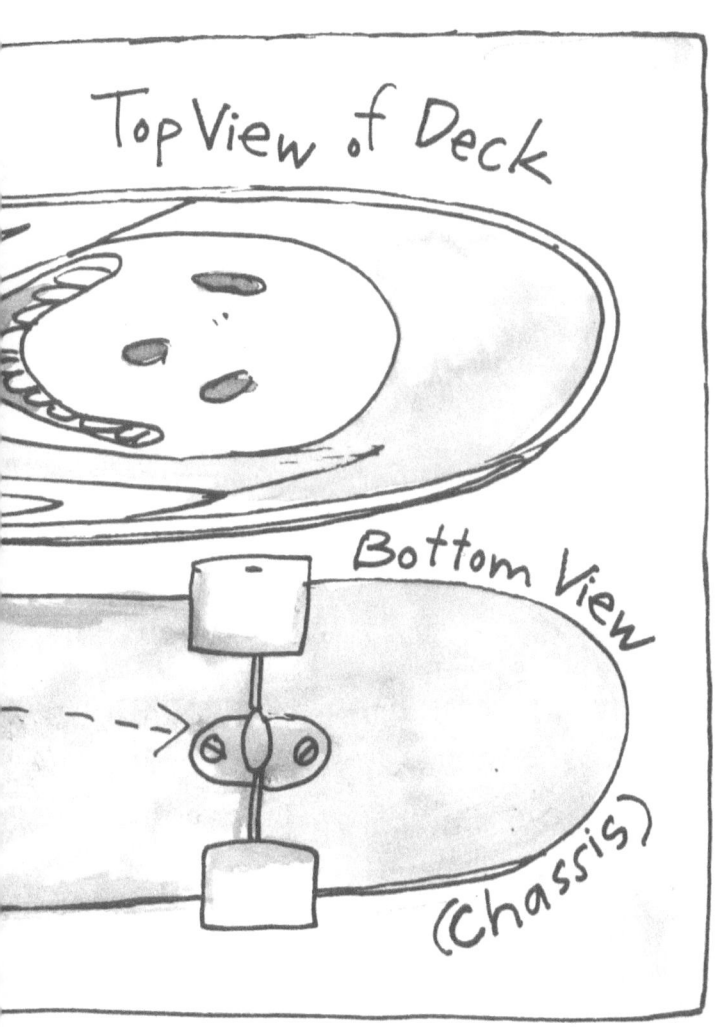

Q & A with Toocool
He Answers His Own Questions

🛹 **Toocool, what makes you the skateboard standout you are?**
I think it's the fact that I am the best at every sport I have ever tried. This makes it easy for me to become a champion at anything I put my mind to.

Are there any special skills you need to be a skateboarder?
You need to have great balance. You have to feel the need for speed like I do. You shouldn't be scared of falling off your board. If you want to skate as well as I do, you must have no fear.

What makes your board so much better than other kids' boards?
I take good care of my board. I keep the trucks well oiled. I never leave my board out at night. My deck is spotless.

Also, I keep my board away from Dog. He chewed one of the wheels once. Never again.
A chewed wheel is useless.

Where do you get your safety gear?

I use my bike helmet for my head. I wear Dad's gardening gloves for my hands or, if Dad's gardening, I wear my ski gloves. I also tape cushions from the couch to my elbows and knees.

You can buy special elbow pads, kneepads, and wrist guards, but my gear suits me.

Have you ever hurt yourself skateboarding?

Yes, before I became a standout I skinned my knees and my elbows, but I handled the pain well. Now that I have good safety gear, I don't get hurt.

Do you like skateboarding better than surfing?

It's not easy to choose between the two. I'm a surfing pro and a skateboarding standout. I am loyal to both sports, although once I started surfing, I knew I would need something to do when I was far away from the waves.

On my next summer vacation, I am taking my skateboard to the beach so I can skate around the campground. It's going to be a surf and skate vacation. Cool!

Skateboard Quiz
How Much Do You Know about Skateboarding?

🛹 **Q1** What is a bowl?
A. Something you mix a cake in.
B. A place for skateboarding.
C. A type of haircut. *D.* All of the above.

🛹 **Q2** What is an ollie?
A. A type of candy. *B.* The first trick you learn on a skateboard.
C. A skating award.

Q3 What is a kick flip?
A. The way you start a motorcycle. *B.* The same as an ollie but you kick the board in the air and land with bent knees. *C.* An excellent karate move.

Q4 What is a nose grind?
A. When the front truck of your board grinds into the path. *B*. When you fall off your bike and land on your nose. *C.* A tough homework assignment.

Q5 Should you wear a helmet?
A. Only if you don't have a hard head. *B.* Always. *C.* Only if you are new to skateboarding.

Q6 How do you make your skateboard go faster?
A. Push harder. **B.** Attach a motor. **C.** Oil the wheels.

Q7 What is a board slide?
A. When you use the middle of the board to slide down a rail.
B. When you slip and slide off your board. **C**. A new type of slide in TC Park.

Q8 What is a flip?
A. What you do when you lose your temper. **B.** Turning a pancake in the frying pan. **C.** When your board does a 360° flip.

Q9 What is impossible?
A. Copying Toocool. **B.** The TC Twist. **C.** Building another Scott Ramp. **D.** All of the above.

Q10 Who is the world's greatest skateboard guru?
A. Scott. **B.** Toocool. **C.** Mr. Lopez.

ANSWERS
1 D.   *2* B.   *3* B.
4 A.   *5* B.   *6* A.
7 A.   *8* C.   *9* D.
10 B.

If you got ten questions right, you're ready for the TC Twist. If you got more than five right, keep trying. If you got fewer than five right, quit while you're ahead.

Toocool

Golfing Giant

Toocool has the perfect swing, but where will the ball end up? Beware of the golfing giant!

Titles in the Toocool series

Slam Dunk Magician
Fishing Fanatic
BMX Champ
Surfing Pro
Tennis Ace
Skateboard Standout
Golfing Giant
Football Legend
Sonic Mountain Bike
Supreme Sailor

Gocart Genius
Invincible Iron Man
Soccer Superstar
Baseball's Best
Water Slide Winner
Beach Patrol
Rodeo Cowboy
Space Captain
Daredevil on Ice
Discus Dynamo

www.ingramcontent.com/pod-product-compliance
Lightning Source LLC
Chambersburg PA
CBHW021124080526
44587CB00010B/640